What if we do

nOthing?

ENDANGERED SPECIES

Sean Sheehan

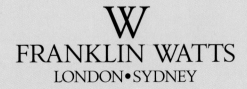

FRANKLIN WATTS
LONDON • SYDNEY

First published in 2009 by Franklin Watts

Copyright © 2009 Arcturus Publishing Limited

Franklin Watts
338 Euston Road
London NW1 3BH

Franklin Watts Australia
Level 17/207 Kent Street, Sydney, NSW 2000

Produced by Arcturus Publishing Limited,
26/27 Bickels Yard, 151-153 Bermondsey Street,
London SE1 3HA

The right of Sean Sheehan to be identified as
the author of this work has been asserted by
him in accordance with the Copyright, Designs
and Patents Act 1988.

Series concept: Alex Woolf
Editor: Alex Woolf
Designer: Phipps Design
Picture researcher: Alex Woolf

A CIP catalogue record for this book is available
from the British Library.

Dewey Decimal Classification Number: 333.95'22

ISBN 978 0 7496 8742 7

Printed in China

Franklin Watts is a division of Hachette
Children's Books, an Hachette Livre UK company.
www.hachettelivre.co.uk

Picture Credits
Corbis: 5 (Yann Arthus-Bertrand), 6 (Michael and Patricia Fogden),
8 (Gustavo Gilabert/Corbis Saba), 9 (Wolfgang Kaehler), 10 (Colin
McPherson), 13 (Yvette Cardozo), 16 (DLILLC), 19 (Jeffrey L
Rotman), 21 (Stephen Frink), 22 (Ed Kashi), 26 (Ron Sachs/Corbis
Sygma), 29 (epa), 31 (Alex Hofford/epa), 32 (Bobby Yip/Reuters), 34
(W Perry Conway), 37 (Layne Kennedy), 39 (Momatiuk/Eastcott), 41
(Roger Tidman), 43 (Paul A Souders), 45 (Torsten
Blackwood/Pool/epa).
NASA: 23 (Jeff Schmaltz, MODIS Rapid Response Team,
NASA/GSFC).
Shutterstock: cover bottom left (Miranda van der Kroft), cover
bottom right (Tom C Amon), cover background (aliciahh), 15
(Christian Riedel), 25 (Simone van den Berg), 30 (Clive Gibson), 35
(Sam Chadwick), 36 (Pete Carron).

Cover pictures
bottom left: The gorilla lives in the tropical forests and mountains
of Africa. It is threatened by habitat destruction, commercial
hunting and poaching.
top right: The red-eyed tree frog is a native of lowland rainforests
in Central America. They are captured for zoos and for pets and
their habitat is threatened by deforestation.
background: Leopard fur. Leopards are on the 'Red List' of
endangered species, threatened by habitat loss and hunting.

Every attempt has been made to clear copyright. Should there be
any inadvertent omission, please apply to the publisher for
rectification.

Contents

CHAPTER 1

Rainforests Under Threat

It is 2025 and, despite worldwide protests, the logging of the Brazilian rainforests continues. This has caused yet another winter of floods and landslides. Rivers have become polluted and their banks destroyed in the flooding. The logging of so much of the Brazilian rainforest has wiped out an incalculable number of plants, including several that had proved useful in the treatment of cancer and other serious illnesses. Hundreds of species of animals and insects have also been wiped out. In the few isolated areas of forest that remain, animals and plants are dying as their food sources and habitats are lost. Species such as fruit-eating bats, which once played a vital role in spreading seeds in the forest, have disappeared. That makes it even harder for the forest to grow back. Amphibians such as the harlequin frog, which once provided food for predators and kept insect numbers down, are long gone. Their thin skins made them vulnerable to a disease-carrying fungus, which has spread due to global warming. The forest's greatest predator, the jaguar, is gone from Brazilian forests, hunted to extinction by farmers.

The rainforest

The world's rainforests are situated around the equator in South and Central America, Asia and Africa. Rainforests have a hot, humid climate. They once covered 14 per cent of the planet but now cover only 2 per cent. Nevertheless, they provide a habitat (an environment offering food, shade, shelter and protection) for half of all known species of flora and fauna (plants and animals). Because the rainforests are shrinking as a result of human activities, many of these species are now under threat.

What is an endangered species?

When the number of individuals in a species becomes very low and the species is at risk of dying out, it is known as an endangered

A section of the Brazilian rainforest has been cut down for its timber and to make space for cash crops. Similar sights can be seen in many of the world's rainforests.

species. This has happened to many species over the course of earth's history, and many have suffered extinction (the death of a species). Over millions of years, as conditions on earth have changed, plants and animals have either adapted or become extinct. Change has usually happened very gradually, giving time for each species to adapt.

However, some changes have been so enormous and so sudden that only a few species of plants and animals survived. One such change occurred around 65 million years ago, killing off the dinosaurs. It was probably caused by a meteor colliding with the earth or an enormous volcanic eruption that led to rapid climate change. The most recent of these sudden changes was the last Ice Age, when large numbers of big animals such as the sabre-toothed tiger and the mammoth became extinct. Since the ice sheets did not reach as far as the equator, many of the rainforest animals survived.

In the last few hundred years, human behaviour has begun to create a threat of mass species extinction even more sudden and destructive than the last Ice Age. No one knows how many species have become extinct, but some scientists suggest that, as each hectare of rainforest is cleared, as many as 140 extinctions of tiny insects and plants could be occurring every day.

ENDANGERED NUMBERS

So far, scientists concerned with extinction have examined only about 40,000 of the estimated 1.5 million species of flora and fauna that exist on earth. The following percentages show how many of those are in danger of becoming extinct:

- 25 per cent of mammals
- 12 per cent of birds
- 33 per cent of amphibians
- 52 per cent of insects
- 51 per cent of reptiles
- 33 per cent of conifer trees
- 73 per cent of flowering plants

Some scientists estimate that half of all species currently surviving will be extinct by 2100.

Ecosystems

All of the earth's animals and plants depend on one another for their survival. Large predators, like tigers, need smaller animals for food. Smaller animals need plants or insects for food. Plant life depends on the large predators to keep down the numbers of grazing animals and prevent overgrazing. In this way, groups of plants and animals live in interdependent communities, which we call ecosystems. The needs of all the species within an ecosystem are held in a delicate balance. If one key species is taken out, the whole system may be threatened.

This harlequin frog, an endangered creature of the Amazon rainforest, displays its warning colours to deter predators. However, this does not offer protection against threats such as pollution, fungal disease and trout, introduced to the rivers where harlequins spawn.

In the rainforest, bats and birds distribute seeds, the harlequin frog and other amphibians keep down insect numbers, and the jaguar preys on smaller mammals that might otherwise overgraze the forest floor.

One example of the complex interdependence of species within an ecosystem involves the hyacinth macaw. This beautiful, endangered bird of the Brazilian rainforest depends on one of its own predators, the toco toucan, to provide its home. Toucans hollow out holes in tree trunks for their nests and the macaw uses abandoned toucan nests in just one rare species of tree, the manduvi tree, for its own nests. If the toucan or the manduvi tree, itself dependent on other species for pollination and seed dispersal, become extinct, the macaw will lose its habitat and follow them into extinction.

GLOBAL WARMING

The earth is getting warmer. We notice it in warmer summers, earlier springs, more violent weather and the melting of glaciers. Part of global warming is probably natural - the earth's climate has changed many times over millions of years and it is likely that we are now experiencing another period of change. However, most scientists agree that human activity is causing global warming to proceed at a faster pace. One reason for this is the release of so-called 'greenhouse gases', which prevent heat from escaping the earth's atmosphere. One of these gases is carbon dioxide, which is released when we burn wood, coal, oil or natural gas. Rainforests, along with the ocean, play an important role in taking carbon dioxide, as well as heat, out of the atmosphere. As trees make new leaves, they absorb carbon dioxide and heat energy from the sun and lock them away for as long as the tree survives. Trees also produce oxygen - vital for humans and animals - as a waste gas. As we cut down the rainforests, their capacity to absorb heat and carbon dioxide - and to produce oxygen - is diminished.

Why the rainforest is shrinking

Honduran mahogany was once widespread throughout Central and South America. Today it is threatened with extinction because it has been cut down and used throughout the world for hardwood furniture. Logging – cutting down trees for wood – is a profitable industry in the rainforest. Rainforest hardwoods are used around the world for furniture, housebuilding and paper making. Most logging is unregulated by governments. The loggers cut down everything in their path in order to get at the valuable wood. Their machines cause ruts, damage the soil structure, pollute rivers and destroy habitats. Burning the unused branches causes forest fires and exposes animals to danger from the fire and from hunters. Controlled logging, where only the valuable wood is removed, is less harmful but still destructive.

Large areas of rainforest are also cleared by agricultural companies in order to graze cattle or grow cash crops (crops grown for sale, not personal consumption) such as soya, used for cattle feed. The environmental organization Greenpeace reports that in Brazil alone, between August and December 2007, some 7,000 square kilometres of rainforest were cut down to provide land for cash crops. Rainforest soil is thin and, after the first cash crop, large amounts of fertilizer must be added to maintain the soil's fertility. It is cheaper to cut down more forest than to import expensive artificial fertilizer, so more forest is cut down every year.

Other threats to the rainforest come from mining and from damming the rivers for electricity. Along the Amazon River, open-cast mining is carried out, in which land is cut away in order to extract precious minerals. Stripping away the soil exposes poisonous chemicals such as sulphur, which are then washed into the river, killing aquatic life. Dams destroy the habitats of fish and plants. One animal threatened by both mining and damming on the Amazon is the pink river dolphin. The pollution destroys its prey and the dams isolate communities of dolphins along stretches of the river.

(opposite) In a cleared area at the edge of this rainforest on the Caribbean island of Dominica, banana plants are grown. Instead, the planters could have collected fruits and nuts from the forest to sell.

(below) A freshly cleared area of the Brazilian rainforest burns. Ranchers, farmers and timber companies slash and burn large areas each year. In the background is a plantation of palms, being grown as a cash crop.

SOME RAINFOREST FACTS

- 37 per cent of medicines used in the West today are derived from rainforest plants, including treatments for leukaemia, breast cancer and asthma.

- 70 per cent of plants from which cancer-treating drugs have been made have come from rainforests.

- 90 per cent of traditional medicines used by the people of rainforests have not yet been tested for use in modern medicine.

- One hectare of rainforest absorbs a tonne of carbon dioxide each year.

- Every second, an area of rainforest the size of two sports grounds is logged somewhere in the world.

- Clearing and burning rainforest accounts for as much as 25 per cent of the carbon released into the air.

Saving the rainforests

It is estimated that five centuries ago 10 million people lived in rainforests. Today, fewer than 40,000 rainforest dwellers survive. They have valuable knowledge about the forest that may soon be lost to everyone. These people have been able to live in the rainforest without harming it. Governments could learn from them how to protect the forests. But this can only happen if the rainforest dwellers survive.

One way of preventing more rainforest destruction is to maintain the fertility of the land that is already cleared. This will encourage farmers not to abandon it and cut down more trees for newly fertile land. Some crops, such as bananas and coffee, benefit from the shade provided by older trees, so some cash crop farming could be encouraged within the outskirts of the rainforest. Other trees, such as the brazil nut tree, provide a valuable crop and will only survive in the deep cover of the forest.

A native of the Amazon collects seeds from the annatto tree. The seeds are used as food colouring, dye, in cosmetics and in medicine. Rainforest peoples have traditionally lived from fruits and vegetables harvested from the rainforest.

Builders and carpenters could find alternatives to rainforest hardwoods for making houses and furniture. Governments could ban the import of hardwoods unless they are from managed forests where the removal of valuable trees is limited, leaving enough young trees and plants for the forest to grow back. They could – as some governments are already doing – pay landowners not to cut down their forests.

Some experts have suggested that farming the rainforest itself – gathering its fruits and seeds and medicines – could be worth more per hectare of land than logging, cash cropping or mining.

DEBATE

You are in charge
You live in a small community in South America. A logging company wants to cut down the rainforest that surrounds your village. A travel company wants to run tours from your village for bird-watching groups interested in spotting rare species. Both need permission from the village. Some people favour the logging company because they want to use the cleared land to grow bananas, oil palm trees, and soya to make money that your village desperately needs. What's your position?

- You would allow the logging company to clear cut the forest. Raising cash crops is the best way to use the land.

- You would allow the logging company to take down some trees, but only if the company agrees to use selective logging.

- You would deny the logging company permission. The tour group will provide a new source of income for the village that won't damage the rainforest.

What other things might the village consider doing to make money that would not harm the rainforest?

CHAPTER 2

African Wildlife

It is 2025. In Kenya, an African country that depends on tourism as a major source of its income, news reports confirm that a gang of criminals entered the largest national park armed with guns. Disguised as tourists, the gang set out to hunt the rare breeding groups of black rhinos that made the park so famous. They killed the entire herd, taking their horns in order to sell them on the black market. It is thought there are now no more black rhinos in Africa.

Africa

Africa covers six per cent of the earth's surface and contains 14 per cent of the human population. Its 46 countries include some of the poorest nations in the world. Africa is also home to some of the world's most varied wildlife. The savannahs – areas of grassland and brush – cover around 13 million square kilometres and support an enormous diversity of flora and fauna. About 850 African animal species are considered endangered and those are just the ones that have been discovered and assessed. The black rhino and the mountain gorilla are critically endangered animals, at risk of extinction in the next few years. Others, less well known to the world, such as the Marungu sunbird of Zaire or the African wild ass, are seriously at risk from loss of habitat.

Africa also has the largest and oldest of the world's deserts: the Sahara, where, for example, the endangered slender horned gazelle is hunted for its horn. African

THE RED LIST

The World Conservation Union (WCU) is an international organization that was set up in 1948. Each year it assesses the threat to endangered species by counting or estimating the number of as many species as possible. This is called the Red List. The list places animals in various degrees of endangerment according to the numbers still surviving and the potential threats to their survival. African animals on the Red List include:

- African elephant (vulnerable)
- African wild dog (endangered)
- black-footed cat (vulnerable)
- black rhinoceros (critically endangered)
- bonobo (endangered)
- cheetah (endangered)
- lion (vulnerable)
- mountain gorilla (critically endangered)
- mountain zebra (endangered)
- pygmy hippopotamus (endangered)
- riverine rabbit (critically endangered)

coastlines provide a vast range of habitats from coastal lagoons to mangrove swamps, river deltas and marshland. The critically endangered Mediterranean monk seal, perhaps numbering as few as 500, inhabits the Saharan coast. The inland rainforests are the second largest in the world. Africa's highest mountain, Kilimanjaro, is also home to many endangered animals, including leopards, elephants and the rare Abbott's duiker, a type of antelope.

Ecotourism

Tourism has had a beneficial effect on African wildlife. Nature reserves and safari parks employ local people as rangers or as staff in the tourist lodges. Locals are also able to sell handicrafts to visitors. The income provides a living for people who might otherwise see the wildlife, such as elephants and lions, as a threat or as food. The income earned by the parks also helps pay for the cost of protecting the animals. Another benefit of the parks is that when visitors see the different animals in the wild, they are more likely to be convinced of the need to protect them. In this way, many of Africa's wild animals owe their survival to 'ecotourism'.

A guest at a wildlife park in Kenya photographs a giraffe in its natural habitat. Promoters of ecotourism hope that this kind of experience will give visitors an awareness of how important the survival of the world's wild places are.

Animals versus big business

Africa is rich in valuable gems, minerals and metals, and this has attracted international mining companies to the continent. But open-cast mining destroys the habitats of animals and plants. Rivers are dammed to supply water to mining camps and this causes habitat loss to some highly endangered small animals that depend on the river systems. One example is the hippo of Ghana, whose habitat will be completely flooded by the Bui Dam project, built to power an aluminium-processing plant. The mining of minerals such as diamonds can expose chemicals such as sulphur, which are dumped back into the waterways, harming aquatic life.

Large profits can be made from logging valuable hardwoods such as sapelli, which is harvested from the forests of the Congo river basin in the Democratic Republic of Congo. The logging companies build roads to reach previously inaccessible areas. These allow in hunters, attracted by the high prices paid by rich individuals and companies for ivory, rhino horn, animal skins and other animal products. African governments are often torn between economic and environmental concerns. Mining and logging bring in money that their countries need. Yet they know these industries threaten endangered species and their habitats.

MADAGASCAR

The island of Madagascar lies off the south-east coast of Africa. It contains some of the rarest creatures in the world, many of which have only ever existed on the island. Its forests once covered almost the whole island. Today, they have been reduced to about 15 per cent of the land area, and 11 species of animals are on the WCU Red List. The loss of habitat caused by forest and bamboo clearance for farmland poses the greatest threat to these animals. The government of Madagascar, in recognition of the danger of species extinction, has begun creating wildlife reserves. It hopes that this will create employment and income for the people of Madagascar, as well as helping to protect the island's animals.

Animal versus human needs

Another threat to the animals of the African wildernesses are the needs of the growing human population. Some experts estimate that Africa's population may double by 2050. Cities, towns and villages are expanding and the need for agricultural land grows in proportion to the population. Throughout sub-Saharan Africa, grassland is being lost to the cultivation of cash crops and farmsteads, while bush land and forests are being cut down for firewood and to clear fresh land for farming.

As humans and wildlife move closer together, animals such as elephants and the larger predators can start to pose a threat to farmers, their homes and crops. Sometimes animals are hunted by villagers seeking safety for their families. As the human population grows, people are also killing increasing numbers of wild animals, such as apes and zebras, for food.

THE GREATER BAMBOO LEMUR

The greater bamboo lemur is one of the most endangered animals in the world. This monkey-like creature's only food source is the giant bamboo, a plant that is being cut down at a rapid rate to make way for farmland. It lives in one area of southern Madagascar and its numbers are estimated at about 1,000. It is one of the rarest animals in the world.

The ring-tailed lemur, although not as threatened as the greater bamboo lemur, is also in danger of extinction. The ring-tailed lemur inhabits forested areas in south-west Madagascar, many of which have been cleared. It also exists in zoos worldwide.

Pygmy hippo

Many of Africa's large mammals are under threat due to habitat loss and poaching. The pygmy hippo lives in West Africa, but only in the forested river areas of Liberia and around the Niger delta. The WCU estimates their numbers in the wild at only 2,000 to 3,000. The pygmy hippo is threatened by a number of developments. Liberia's rainforest has been heavily logged, leaving fewer areas for the hippo to survive in. The nation was also at war almost continuously from 1989 to 2003. This disrupted food supplies for many people, and the pygmy hippo was hunted as a source of meat.

The black rhino was once a thriving species throughout central and eastern Africa. However, the high value of its horn has made it a target for illegal hunting and vulnerable to extinction.

THE MEDICINAL VALUE OF BLACK RHINO HORN

Black rhino horn is highly valued in traditional Chinese medicine. Experiments by scientists show that very large quantities of the horn can reduce fever. An aspirin, however, works just as well and no rhinos are killed to make aspirin.

Black rhinoceros

The black rhinoceros, unlike the pygmy hippo, can survive in a variety of habitats, including semi-desert, savannah and forests, yet its numbers have also fallen drastically. There are now as few as 3,700, living almost entirely within game reserves. The danger to the black rhino is from poachers (people who hunt illegally), who can sell its horn for large sums through illegal trade (see panel).

In 1973, the Convention on International Trade in Endangered Species (CITES) was signed by 63 countries. The countries agreed, among other things, to ban trade in all rhino products. Unfortunately, the ban has increased the price of rhino horn on the black (illegal) market, driving poachers to ever-greater efforts to obtain it. Some African countries, such as Namibia and Zimbabwe, have removed their rhinos' horns so that the poachers will leave them alone. Other countries carry out a shoot-to-kill policy on poachers. Zoos around the world have made their own efforts to preserve the black rhino through captive breeding programmes. The United States has imposed trade sanctions against countries such as Taiwan, where the trade, while illegal, is still widespread.

DEBATE

You are in charge

The government of an African country is considering letting a mineral mine build a dam on one of its major rivers. The dam will flood hundreds of square kilometres of a national park, including several areas that are known to be the only habitat of a rare plant. You are a member of a local environmental group. Which argument do you think will be most effective to persuade the government to stop the dam project?

- Workers in the national park will lose their jobs and homes. The national park brings in lots of money from tourism.
- Where the dam floods forested areas, the water will become polluted with rotting debris and important habitats will be lost forever.
- Water supplies to a neighbouring country will be affected.

CHAPTER 3

The Oceans

It is 2025 and the World Conservation Union (WCU) has added herring, tuna and mullet to its list of critically endangered species. Cod is now extinct. Fishing fleets around the world lie idle as going out to sea is no longer profitable. Fishing villages are abandoned. Their inhabitants pack up and head to cities in search of work and food. Japan, Norway and Russia send out whaling fleets in an effort to use whale meat as a replacement for fish.

Endangered oceans

The ocean is as endangered as the creatures that live in it. It is a complex ecosystem containing many interdependent species. Fish, shellfish, seabirds, whales, turtles, seaweed, algae, plankton and coral reefs all depend on each other for survival. Marine life has been extensively researched since 2005 for inclusion in the World Conservation Union Red List of endangered species. In 2007, several kinds of coral and several sharks and rays were added to the endangered list.

Even more worrying in terms of the world as a whole, several kinds of algae were also added to the list. Algae are the lungs of the ocean in the same way that the rainforests are the lungs of the land. Algae take in carbon dioxide and sunlight to reproduce and release oxygen into the atmosphere. They are at the bottom of the ocean's food chain. If algae become endangered, then all the creatures in the food chain are threatened too. Algae and the other inhabitants of the ocean are threatened by pollution, overfishing, global warming, oil exploration and tourism.

The price of fish

Overfishing is currently the biggest threat to marine life. Technological advances and greater demand for fish from an increasing world population has brought some fish to

SOME OCEAN FACTS

- Oceans cover 75 per cent of the earth.
- Fish and shellfish provide about 16 per cent of the world's protein needs.
- Ocean algae may produce as much as 90 per cent of the atmosphere's oxygen.
- The ocean absorbs incalculable amounts of carbon dioxide from the atmosphere.
- It has the potential to provide as-yet-unknown medical products.
- It helps regulate our climate, taking in heat from the sun and releasing it slowly.

near-extinction in certain areas. This, for example, is the case with the Atlantic sturgeon around the coasts of Canada. Since the early 20th century, many countries have established fishing quotas – restrictions on the number of fish that can be caught by fishing fleets. Some have introduced regulations limiting the size of nets to give young and smaller fish the opportunity to escape being caught. In 2007, an international agreement banned bottom trawling, a highly destructive form of fishing, in the South Pacific.

An estimated 27 million tons of sea creatures are killed by trawlers each year by becoming accidentally caught up in the nets. These include sharks, rays, dolphins, turtles and seabirds.

In Massachusetts Bay, cod fishermen clean their catch. In 2000, the World Wildlife Fund (WWF) placed cod on its endangered list, stating that the global cod catch had fallen by 70 per cent since 1970. The WWF claimed that if this trend continued, the world's cod stocks would disappear by 2019.

Whales

Whales are hunted chiefly for their meat. Like other forms of fishing, whale hunting has become more efficient, with bigger ships, stronger harpoons and better detection equipment. Smaller whales get caught up in fishing nets and others are killed by collisions with ships. Five species of whale are considered endangered and many others are at risk. In 1986, nearly 80 countries banned whaling. Since that time, scientists believe that whale numbers have increased. The countries that traditionally hunted whales, such as Greenland, Iceland, Japan and Norway, want the ban lifted. A 2006 report commissioned by the Convention on Migratory Species concluded that whale-watching trips for tourists can bring in much higher profits than whale hunting.

Polar bears

Polar bears, the world's largest land carnivores, live on the Arctic sea ice. Polar bears number over 20,000, enough to keep them off the endangered section of the WCU Red List. Nevertheless, they too are threatened, not directly by humans but indirectly. Polar bears hunt in the autumn, winter and spring, catching seals, fish and other marine creatures. In summer, when the ice fields melt, they return to the land mass of the Arctic and live off their body fat.

Each year, however, due to global warming, the ice recedes by about 3 per cent and this reduces the polar bears' hunting grounds. The higher temperatures melt their dens, exposing their young to the weather and predators. Scientists estimate that the polar bears' habitat will be gone in 100 years. Since 1972, the United States has banned the hunting of polar bears. Russia allows limited hunting by indigenous (native) groups. Canada and Greenland, the other countries with polar bear populations, allow polar bear hunting for sport.

Coral

Coral are tiny animals related to sea anemones and jellyfish. Corals cover about 260,000 square kilometres of the ocean floor in shallow, nutrient-poor seas around the equator. It is estimated that about

THE DUGONG

The dugong is a marine mammal similar to a manatee. It lives in the shallow waters around the coral reefs of Australia, East Africa and the islands of Indonesia. It has been hunted for centuries for its meat, skin, bones and oil. Many of its habitats are now protected and the total population of dugongs is thought to be about 160,000. Nevertheless, the dugong's survival is still threatened by hunting, habitat destruction and by entanglement in nets and collisions with boats.

500,000 marine species live among the coral reefs. People are threatening the coral reefs in various ways. Some hunt fish in them with chemicals that destroy the corals. Tourist resorts are often built along coasts where coral reefs are close to shore, polluting the waters. Also, global warming is causing the gradual acidification of the ocean. As carbon dioxide from the air dissolves in the water of the sea, it forms an acid called carbonic acid. More carbon dioxide, released by the burning of fossil fuels, causes the sea to become increasingly acidic. The acid eats into the coral and into the millions of shellfish that live among the coral. About 10 per cent of the world's coral reefs are already dead and another 60 per cent are endangered. Many countries with coral reefs in their waters have created marine parks in order to protect them.

This bleached staghorn coral is a victim of global warming. Higher sea temperatures have killed the algae that live in the coral and which it depends upon for its survival.

A toxic soup

Until 2006, when international controls came into effect, millions of tons of waste were dumped in the ocean each year. These included by-products of oil refineries, nuclear waste, agricultural waste and sewage. All this pollution has taken its toll on fish numbers and has led to high levels of toxic chemicals in the bigger fish.

When sewage encounters algae, the nutrients in the sewage cause the algae to multiply far beyond normal levels. This causes algae blooms, when so much algae develops on the surface of the sea that it deprives

Pollution from this gas and oil plant in Nigeria has caused fish numbers in the area to fall. The village beside the plant depends on fish such as the bonga fish for food and income. While these fish are not yet threatened with extinction, the local community, which depended on clean waters and a good catch, is suffering.

FOOD CHAINS

The smallest creatures in the sea are known as phytoplankton. These are tiny plants that use sunlight, nutrients from the ocean and carbon dioxide to reproduce. They are eaten by tiny marine animals called zooplankton. These get eaten in turn by bigger creatures such as fish, which are eaten by larger fish or other marine creatures such as turtles or whales. In polluted seas, each creature in the food chain will absorb pollutants during the course of its life. The animals at the top of the chain, such as whales, tuna or sharks, have the greatest quantity of pollutants in their systems, because everything they have eaten has also absorbed pollutants. This may affect their growth and reproduction, and may ultimately kill them.

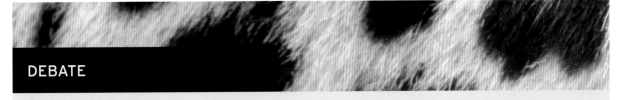

DEBATE

You are in charge

You are a member of a group that regulates whaling. Several groups have asked you to allow them to begin hunting whales that have recently been removed from the endangered species list. Although the whales have increased in number, their populations remain low. Which groups, if any, are you most likely to permit to hunt whales again?

- Small groups of Inuits who depend on whales to provide food, heating, clothing and cash.
- Commercial whalers who use modern fishing techniques.
- Countries such as Norway, which claim that whaling is a vital part of their culture.

What arguments might you expect to hear from environmental groups and whale watching businesses about this proposal to allow more hunting? What's your opinion?

other marine life of oxygen and creates dead areas. In 2004, nearly 150 dead zones were observed in an aerial survey. One of the dead zones was over 180,000 square kilometres in size. Fortunately, these dead zones are not permanent. The excess nutrients are eventually consumed or dispersed. Since 1975 international regulations have restricted the amount and type of waste material that can be released into the sea. By 2001, 78 countries had agreed to abide by these rules. They hope this will prevent more blooms from occurring.

This algae bloom (seen here as a light blue area) off the coast of France and Britain was so big that a satellite was able to photograph it. The bloom was probably caused by sewage or chemical fertilizers leaking into the sea.

CHAPTER 4

Asia's Animals

The year is 2025. Orang-utans have become extinct in the wild. They lost their habitat with the destruction of the South-East Asian rainforest and were hunted for sale in the exotic pet trade. The last survivors, numbering only 18, have been collected together at the Sepilok orang-utan sanctuary in Sabah, Borneo. Conservationists hope that successful breeding at Sepilok will increase the number of orang-utans. Scientists also plan to begin experimenting with cloning to further boost the orang-utan population. Visitors to the Sepilok sanctuary will need to book years in advance and pay high entrance fees to see the orang-utans.

Gentle giants of the rainforest

Orang-utans once inhabited forested areas in China, Thailand, Malaysia, Borneo and Indonesia. Gentle, funny, sociable creatures, they are the largest tree-dwelling animal in the world and the only great ape to live outside of Africa. Today they live in two areas: Borneo and the Indonesian island of Sumatra. Present numbers are less than 60,000 and, because their habitat is under increasing threat from logging, they are expected to become extinct in the wild by the mid-2020s. Female orang-utans produce, on average, only one infant every seven years. The young stay with their mother, learning how to survive, until age ten or even older. As well as the danger posed by logging, orang-utans are under threat from the illegal pet trade.

SEPILOK ORANG-UTAN REHABILITATION CENTRE

Loggers often kill adult orang-utans and take the babies to sell as pets, although this is now illegal. Some of these orphaned orang-utans are rescued and taken to the Sepilok Orang-utan Rehabilitation Centre. Based in a tiny reserve of 43 square kilometres in the north of Borneo, Sepilok shelters the orphans until they learn to fend for themselves. The tame, helpless animals are gradually taken deeper into the forest as they learn to find food, build nests and avoid human contact. It is one of only two places left in the wild where orang-utans can be seen in their natural habitat.

EXOTIC PETS

Annual figures for animals captured and sold as pets each year are as follows:

- 4 million birds
- 640,000 reptiles
- 40,000 primates
- 350 million tropical fish

The annual profits for the exotic pet trade are around US$6 billion. Most reptiles die within a year of capture, and other pets are abandoned or suffer in captivity. Many species carry diseases that can be transmitted to humans or livestock.

An orang-utan mother has her hands full with two babies to rear. If they are female, they will stay with her for ten years or more. Sons will go off to find new mates at around age ten. A female orang-utan will only have about four or five babies in her lifetime.

Asia and its wildlife

Asia is the world's largest and most densely populated continent. It contains more than 60 per cent of the world's population and nearly 30 per cent of the earth's total land area. India and China, two of the world's most populous countries, are undergoing huge economic growth. This has led to an expansion of their towns and cities. Wilderness areas have been developed for agriculture or settlement, threatening wildlife habitats. As a result, both countries are home to some seriously endangered species, including the tiger, the giant panda and the Asian elephant.

These pandas, born in the China Research and Conservation Centre for the Giant Panda in Wolong, China, are currently living at the National Zoo in Washington, DC, USA. They have produced one cub during their stay at the zoo.

26

Most of the world's illegal trade in endangered animals takes place in Asia. Many of these animals, such as tigers and rhinos, are highly prized in traditional forms of medicine.

Giant pandas

One of the most well known of all endangered species is the giant panda. Conservationists estimate that between 2,000 and 3,000 remain in the wild. Pandas are protected under the Convention on International Trade in Endangered Species (CITES) agreement (see panel) and are on the WCU Red List. The panda's chief source of food, bamboo, is very poor in nutrients and pandas must eat up to 38 kilogrammes of bamboo every day. About once every decade, the bamboo plant suddenly produces flowers, then dies away, depriving pandas of food. If they don't find an alternative source of bamboo, many pandas can starve. Pandas, like orang-utans, breed slowly, so their numbers are not easily restored after such a loss.

For many years, China attempted to protect giant pandas by bringing as many as possible into captivity. The government has created 40 reserves for giant pandas, removing human residents from these areas. Zoos in other countries can hire pandas for a period of ten years at a cost of US$1 million or more per year. The zoos must agree to return to China any baby pandas born during that time, once they are three years old. The United States has passed a law that prevents zoos from hiring pandas unless most of the fee goes to panda conservation in China.

The problem faced by conservationists is that pandas in zoos and reserves have generally failed to reproduce. Also, many of the panda cubs that were born in captivity died, probably because of the mother's inexperience or poor handling by the zoo keepers. Chinese conservationists have been researching ways of improving panda cub survival rates. Their efforts appear to be bearing fruit: a 2006 survey suggests that the numbers of giant pandas, both in the wild and in captivity, are increasing.

CITES

Since 1973, an international agreement has been in place to regulate trade in endangered species. CITES (the Convention on International Trade in Endangered Species of Wild Fauna and Flora) sets out certain rules for member states to follow, banning or controlling trade in 5,000 species of animals and 28,000 species of plants and their products. The treaty has now been signed by 172 countries and has probably saved many wild creatures from extinction. CITES makes a positive contribution to the preservation of wildlife by banning countries from trading in certain species.

Asian elephants

Tamed and trained Asian elephants are fairly common in India, Sri Lanka, Vietnam, Thailand, Burma, Malaysia and Nepal. In the wild, though, they have become endangered. Their numbers are chiefly threatened by habitat loss rather than hunting. In this they differ from the larger African elephant, which is hunted for its ivory tusks. Only some of the male Asian elephants have tusks and no females have them, so hunting is less profitable. Being migratory animals, moving continuously from one food and water source to another, Asian elephants often come into conflict with humans at roadsides, on railway tracks or in fields, where grain crops are very tempting to them. It is estimated that in India about 200 elephants and 300 humans die each year as a result of encounters between them. There are about 48,000 Asian elephants remaining in the wild and about 15,000 elephants either in game reserves or working in logging operations.

Rewilding the tiger

Tigers were once widespread across Asia, but in modern times they live in small numbers in wildlife reserves where they can be protected from hunters. Tigers are hunted for their skins, used in the fashion industry, and for their meat and bones, used in traditional medicine. Estimates of their numbers in the wild range from 2,500 to 5,000. Four subspecies of tiger are already extinct.

India has 25 wildlife parks, where human settlement is not allowed. The Indian government's Project Tiger scheme, introduced in the 1970s, claims that the Bengal tiger population living in these parks increased steadily until 2007. Numbers began to fall slightly in 2008.

In China, efforts are being made to place some of the tiny numbers of South China tigers back into the wild. The South China tigers held

INBREEDING

When the numbers of a particular species become very low, or the animals live in isolated groups, they begin to inbreed, meaning that breeding occurs between closely related animals. This has happened in many captive breeding programmes in which animals have been traded between one zoo and another for generation after generation. Inbreeding can lead to physical defects in the resulting offspring, such as weakness of bones and blindness. Many of these offspring die young. Using DNA testing, scientists in charge of captive breeding programmes are better able to ensure that animals breed with unrelated mates. The result is stronger, healthier offspring that are more likely to survive in the wild.

in zoos and tiger breeding farms are being sent to special game reserves in Africa. Conservationists hope that the cubs of these tigers will develop as completely wild animals before being returned to China. Unless this project proves successful, experts predict that the South China tiger will become extinct in the near future.

Cathay, a 10-month-old South China tiger, learns to hunt for herself so that she can eventually be returned to the wild. She is one of only about 90 still surviving in the world.

Proboscis monkeys

Proboscis monkeys are a curious-looking species with large overhanging noses, webbed feet and big pot bellies. They live in forested areas along coastlines and rivers, chiefly on the island of Borneo. Proboscis monkeys have been hunted for food and are easy targets because of their lack of shyness and their tendency to travel in groups.

Like their near neighbours, orang-utans, they suffer from the destruction of their habitat as towns expand and new oil palm plantations are established. In just one region of Borneo, the state of Sabah, 16 per cent of the total land area is taken up by oil palm plantations. Sixty per cent of these plantations are on land that was once forest.

New laws in Sabah protect the proboscis monkey, and conservation groups have established several game reserves in the species' preferred habitat. Ecotourism offers hope for the survival of the species, so long as it is managed well. About 7,000 proboscis monkeys still exist in the wild and they are on the WCU Red List.

A proboscis monkey stalks through his native forest in Borneo. In Sarawak, north-east Borneo, the proboscis monkey population declined from 6,500 in 1977 to just 1,000 in 2006, a victim of habitat loss and hunting.

So long and thanks for all the fish

Two of the world's three species of river dolphin live in Asia. They are the Ganges river dolphin and the Yangtze river dolphin, also known as the baiji. The baiji once inhabited about 1,700 kilometres of the Yangtze River in China. Traditionally the river dolphins were treasured, but from the 1950s people were encouraged to hunt the dolphins. Since the 1980s the land along the Yangtze has grown increasingly industrialized and has consequently become very polluted. Water levels have dropped due to climate change and heavy silt deposits. Both the baiji and the fish it fed on have suffered as a result. The baiji also often collided with heavy river traffic and became trapped in fishing nets, accelerating their decline. By 1997 a survey could find only 13 animals. In 2007 conservationists declared the baiji 'functionally extinct', meaning that the population (if any still existed) was no longer able to sustain itself.

The baiji, or Yangtze river dolphin, survived on earth for perhaps 20 million years. A 2007 survey could find no surviving dolphins.

The Ganges river dolphin is doing better than the baiji, with as many as 2,000 surviving in the wild. However, their numbers have also declined due to discharges from factories into the Ganges, dams built across the river systems in India, the silting up of river beds and illegal hunting.

THE SLENDER LORIS

In the forests of Sri Lanka only dwindling numbers of this tiny monkey-like creature survive. Locals regard the slender loris as a sign of bad luck. It is usually killed on sight. The slender loris's parts are used in traditional medicine. Its eyes are considered to possess special healing qualities and its flesh is thought to be a cure for asthma. However, like so many other highly endangered species, the greatest threat to its survival is habitat loss.

The price of a fur coat

The most remote areas of Asia, where animals ought to be safest from human hunters, are the mountainous regions. However, the profits to be made from the body parts of some of the rarer creatures of Asia's mountains tempt many hunters. Snow leopards, whose habitat is the high mountains of Central and South Asia, are hunted for their valuable furs and body parts. A snow leopard fur coat can cost US$50,000 when it is sold in a fashionable store. Snow leopards live in the mountains above the tree line at heights of 2,700 metres above sea level. Between 3,500 and 5,000 remain alive in the wild and their numbers are falling due to illegal hunting of both the leopards and their prey. Experts believe that the snow leopard population is still large enough for the species to survive, so long as demand for its fur does not increase.

These protesters in Causeway Bay, one of Hong Kong's popular shopping areas, cram themselves into a cage to highlight the treatment of animals in the fur trade.

Learning to live with nature

Like the highly endangered plants and animals of other continents and ecosystems, Asian species are threatened by human activity. Population growth and economic expansion have often led to the pollution of wildlife habitats, or their development for agriculture or settlement.

There were few protests when the people of North America and Europe cut down large swathes of forest in the 19th century. At the time few people cared about or understood the damage this would do to the species that lived there. People in Asia wish to live comfortable lives in the same way as people in Europe and North America, so the pressure to grow and expand will continue, with damaging consequences for wildlife.

There is hope for the future, however. People are beginning to realize that their desire for economic prosperity and the needs of wildlife are not necessarily in conflict. Responsibly managed ecotourism, for instance, gives local people a way to make money by conserving the wildlife of their region. Places such as the Bukit Saban resort in Betong, Sarawak, bring tourists interested in wildlife into the forest. Local people lead the treks, entertain the visitors and sell them handicrafts.

DEBATE

You are in charge

Many poor people in Thailand, India and Malaysia live on the borders of forested land, close to the natural habitat of the highly endangered Asian elephant. The settlements break up the elephants' migratory routes, and villagers take the elephants' food sources for firewood. Hungry elephants sometimes attack the villagers' crops and homes. Villagers respond by hunting the elephants. What measures do you think a concerned government might take to help both the villagers and the elephants?

■ Make migratory pathways for the elephants away from human habitation.

■ Offer the villagers compensation and relocation to safer areas with sustainable wood supplies.

■ Build ecotourist lodges in the area to bring in revenue for the threatened villagers.

■ Relocate the elephants to enclosed nature reserves.

What other suggestions could you make to the government?

CHAPTER 5

North American Wildlife

It is 2025. Ecologists have surveyed the environmental impact of the 30 oil fields established in the Arctic National Wildlife Refuge in Alaska in 2010. The survey reveals that significant amounts of toxic substances, including acids, lead, pesticides, solvents and diesel fuel have leaked into the environment from the vehicles and settlements associated with the oil fields. According to wildlife surveys, the endangered musk ox that once inhabited the area has disappeared. Many of the 135 species of birds that migrate through the area, or use it as a nesting site, have declined sharply in numbers. Indigenous people have abandoned their traditional lifestyles and found work chiefly in the oil fields. Two of the fields have ceased producing oil after only 15 years in operation, and the productive life of several others may be drawing to an end.

Alaska

The Arctic National Wildlife Refuge covers nearly 80,000 square kilometres inside the Arctic Circle. It includes six different ecological zones, from coasts and marshlands through upland hills and tundra to vast forests of conifer and broadleaved trees. The refuge sits to the east of Prudhoe Bay oil fields, the largest oil deposits in the United

Some short-tailed albatrosses forage for food in the Arctic National Wildlife Refuge in Alaska. They migrate here from their breeding grounds on the tiny Japanese island of Torishima. There are less than 2,000 short-tailed albatrosses remaining on earth, and the species' survival would be threatened by any damage to the refuge.

The Trans-Alaska Pipeline carries oil from Prudhoe Bay to the ice-free port of Valdez. From there the oil is shipped to refineries around the US. Since it opened, the pipeline and oil tankers have spilled or leaked over a million barrels of oil into the environment.

States, and controversy rages over whether its oil resources should be exploited. The issues for the United States are similar to those faced by African countries, India and states in South-East Asia. A vast, unspoiled piece of land offers enormous short-term profits and economic benefits to the country but at a great cost to the wildlife in the area. The World Conservation Union has registered 11 species of wildlife in the refuge on its Red List, including the short-tailed albatross, Steller's sealion, six species of whale and the leatherback turtle. The WCU is considering adding a further ten species to the list.

UNITED STATES OIL CONSUMPTION

The United States consumes about 20 million barrels of oil a day, some 25 per cent of total world output. Five million barrels come from domestic oil wells in Alaska and other US states. The oil reserves in the Arctic Wildlife Refuge are estimated at between 4 and 11 billion barrels. This is enough to provide 5 per cent of America's oil for 12 to 30 years. Put another way, it would supply all the country's oil demands for 525 days at most. Many conservationists argue that it is not worth damaging the Arctic Wildlife Refuge for such a relatively small amount of oil.

The American bison

Bison, or buffalo as many people call them, are large, grazing mammals that were once a vital food source for the native peoples of North America. Tens of millions of bison ranged from Canada in the north to Mexico in the south. In the 19th century they were hunted almost to extinction, and by the 1890s only tiny herds of bison survived. Their numbers began to increase at the turn of the 20th century as a result of captive breeding programmes. Bison are no longer critically endangered, but many of them have interbred with domestic cattle and very few of the original species remain. The bison in Yellowstone National Park are, in fact, the only surviving pure-bred herd.

As the numbers of the hybrid animals have expanded outside wildlife parks, they have begun competing with domestic livestock for grazing and water. The animals can carry the cattle disease brucellosis, which can infect domestic herds. Also, bison occasionally kill humans when threatened. For these reasons, many farmers have called for action to cull bison. Some American states have begun to permit hunting on a limited scale.

A couple of bison graze at Yellowstone National Park. In winter, the park can only support about 3,000 animals, so each year some of the herd are killed as they wander out of the park and into nearby cattle grazing land.

Wolves

Like many other animals that were regarded as a threat to the human population, some species of wolf were wiped out in the United States by the mid-20th century. Packs of the eastern timber wolf, however, survive in Ontario and Quebec in Canada. There have been some sightings of these animals in the northern United States, and ecologists are studying the possibility of reintroducing them to wilderness areas in the north-east.

In the south-eastern United States the red wolf survives in very small numbers and a few have been reintroduced into the wild from zoos. A small population established in the Great Smoky Mountains in the 1990s failed to survive. It is important that the wolves are resettled in wilderness areas, far from human settlements, as they hunt their prey in packs and can pose a threat to livestock and humans.

By 1980, the red wolf had been completely wiped out in its natural homelands of the south-east United States. Captured animals, bred in captivity, have been released back into the wild. However, the red wolf remains critically endangered, with as few as 250 animals left, most in captivity.

COHABITATION

Many state governments have taken steps to protect their wildlife. They have produced sets of rules for people whose homes are alongside wildlife areas. Here are some survival rules issued by the state of California for humans who live near mountain lions:

- Don't feed deer. It is illegal in California because it will attract mountain lions.
- Make gardens deer-proof by avoiding plants that deer like to eat.
- Keep bushes trimmed to reduce hiding places for mountain lions.
- Don't leave small children or pets outside unattended.
- Provide sturdy fences and covered shelters for livestock.
- Don't allow pets outside between dusk and dawn.
- Feed pets inside the house to avoid attracting small animals, which are possible prey for mountain lions.

Foreign invaders

Some animal species are threatened not by the loss of a key species that they depend on but by the arrival of one. An example of this can be found in the salt marshes of Chesapeake Bay, where a large rat-like creature called the nutria, native to South America, has colonized several salt marshes. The nutria eats marsh plants whose roots form the stable base of the marshlands. As a result, the nutria invaders have caused the erosion of some 7,000 acres of breeding and feeding grounds for fish, crabs and wetland birds, including the endangered black rail. The North American nutria population has expanded enormously. In the salt marshes alone they number in the tens of millions. Ecologists estimate that, in the United States alone, the annual cost of controlling the nutria and other invasive species, and attempting to repair the damage they cause, comes to about US$138 billion.

TOUGH LOVE

The United States has hundreds of wildlife reserves, and many of these protected areas are open to the public. Visitors to these places often pose the primary danger to the wildlife within them. Walkers erode pathways, causing damage to delicate plants. Litter left by visitors enters the food chain. Recreational vehicles, such as all-terrain vehicles and dirt bikes, hit animals, crush plants and pollute the air. Boating enthusiasts introduce alien shellfish attached to the hulls of their boats. Not all the damage is done by visitors, however. Special sprays aimed at stopping brush fires pollute the land and kill native species, allowing in invasive alien plants.

The California condor

This large and critically endangered bird of prey lives around the Grand Canyon and the coastal mountains of California. Condors feed on carrion (dead animals) – often animals that have been shot by humans. The lead pellets in the carrion poisons the condors. Also, many condors collide with power lines. Another major threat to their survival is egg-stealing by humans. By 1989, there were just 25 of these birds left in existence. Conservationists decided to capture every one of them and place them in breeding programmes in zoos. Since 1991, carefully monitored groups have been released back into the wild and are now successfully breeding. By 2008, experts believed the number of California condors had risen to over 300.

This tagged California condor was born in captivity and released into the wild in the Grand Canyon, Arizona. Condors mate for life and the female lays only one egg every two years. It therefore took many years, and careful supervision, for the species to recover following its near extinction.

DEBATE

You are in charge

You are on the governing body of a large national park. Visitors have unthinkingly caused serious damage to the park's environment. They have worn down pathways, causing erosion during rainfall. Their vehicles have hit animals and their noise has frightened birds away from nesting sites. Some individuals have been injured by animal attacks. How do you propose to solve the problems?

- Increase the entrance fees to the park to raise money to repair the damage.

- Limit road access to areas where animals are least likely to be disturbed.

- Ban all vehicles from the park and limit where people can walk on trails.

- Close the park to visitors.

Do you think that national parks should be used by people for recreation or should their main purpose be to preserve and protect the land as a habitat for plants and animals?

CHAPTER 6

Antarctica

It is 2025. Krill, a tiny shrimp-like creature and a vital part of the Antarctica food chain, has been declared endangered. Whales, several species of seal, squid, penguins, albatrosses and other birds, all of which depend on krill, have declined nearly to the point of extinction. The ice caves and sea ice around the coasts of Antarctica are rapidly melting and large blocks of ice are breaking away from the ice mass. Coastal areas around the world are threatened by rising sea levels.

Krill

Antarctic krill live in huge, dense shoals in the waters of the Southern Ocean around Antarctica. They feed on microscopic plants and algae. Algae take in carbon dioxide and water and convert it into sugar, which they use to grow and reproduce, and oxygen which they release back into the atmosphere. The krill digest algae and excrete carbon. The carbon falls to the seabed, where it remains trapped for thousands of years. Krill therefore play an important role in taking carbon out of the atmosphere, reducing global warming.

Krill are the staple food of larger sea creatures, which are in turn eaten by bigger predators. They are one of the most successful and useful creatures on the planet. If they die out, the marine life that depends on them will become extinct.

In recent years some scientists have suggested that krill numbers are already beginning to decrease in the Antarctic. One reason for this is that their breeding and feeding grounds – the shallow waters around the pack-ice coast of Antarctica – have been damaged by the rising temperatures of the Southern Ocean. Another reason is that fishing fleets harvest around 100,000 tonnes

THE IMPORTANCE OF KRILL

Estimated annual consumption of krill by different species:

seals	63-130 million tonnes
whales	34-43 million tonnes
birds	15-20 million tonnes
squid	0-100 million tonnes
fish	0-20 million tonnes

of krill each year. They are used for fish meal, which is used on fish farms, and for human consumption.

If we do nothing, the outlook for krill and the marine life that depends on it is bleak. However, some scientists believe that krill might actually offer a solution to the threat of global warming. Experiments have shown that if small quantities of iron are added to the areas around the Antarctic that are inhabited by krill, the numbers of krill increase. The more krill there are, the more carbon is removed from the atmosphere and sent to the bottom of the ocean.

Krill are an important food source for animals in the Antarctic, including fish, penguins, seals and baleen whales. These animals cannot feed directly on microscopic algae, but the krill converts the energy contained within algae into a form that larger animals can make use of.

Threatened Antarctic species

Antarctica is the southernmost continent on earth. It is also the planet's highest, windiest and driest continent. Its flora is very limited and includes some grasses, lichens, moss and algae. Its animals includes six species of penguin, seals, several species of whale, orcas, dolphins and around 50 species of bird. Antarctica is home to 160 fish species, specially adapted to life at the low temperatures of the continent's coastal waters.

International agreements protect the flora and fauna of Antarctica. The World Conservation Union lists some albatross species and giant southern petrels as endangered. Both birds are scavengers. They follow fishing fleets to snatch fish from their nets and sometimes they become entangled in the long lines used by modern fishing boats.

LONG-LINE FISHING

In recognition that species such as the albatross are threatened by long-line fishing, countries which use this method have agreed on several policies that will help to prevent bird deaths. Long-line fishing boats must:

- Use bird scarers with streamers attached behind their boats.

- Weight their lines so that they sink faster and birds don't see them.

- Dump waste away from the land where there are fewer birds to be attracted to the lines.

- Put their lines out at night when there are fewer birds scavenging.

Emperor penguins are protected by international treaties but are nevertheless considered by some countries to be endangered. This is because of the danger to their habitat as large areas of sea ice disappear each year. Another threat is the decline in the numbers of krill, a key part of their diet.

Also dependent on krill for part of its diet is the fur seal. The fur seal had been hunted to near extinction by the beginning of the 20th century. Commercial seal hunting was banned in the early 1900s, and fur seal numbers have recovered rapidly since then. This may also have been made possible because whale numbers in the Antarctic were reduced by hunting, making it easier for the fur seals to find food.

Governments all around the world are now aware of the importance of keeping this last wilderness safe. The Antarctic Treaty System is a series of international agreements between 46 countries. It regulates fishing, protects flora and fauna and controls the activities of visitors to Antarctica and what they may take there. Dumping waste in Antarctica and in the waters around it is prohibited.

The chief threat to all the species that dwell in Antarctica comes from the rising sea temperatures around the land mass. As temperatures rise, the air around the Antarctic becomes laden with water, and snow forms over the land. This alters the delicately balanced ecosystem of Antarctic plants and animals. Snow may damage penguin nests. Melting ice caves in the pack ice reduced the nursery grounds for young krill. Warmer waters allow new predators to move in and new plants to find a foothold.

A king penguin gives a fur seal a piece of its mind. As sea temperatures rise, affecting the the delicate Antarctic ecosystem, it is likely that these two species will have to compete ever more fiercely for food and territory.

WARMING WATERS

As the sea around Antarctica warms up, it will cause major changes to the local ecosystem. A rise of just 1ºC will allow new predators, previously incapable of surviving the Antarctic winter, to move into the area. Sharks and king crabs will be able to live and hunt in the coastal waters, where they will disrupt centuries-old food chains. The invaders will compete with seabirds, seals and whales for the fish and shellfish that live there.

Bigger or smaller?

Antarctica is a highly complex ecosystem. Some scientists disagree with the commonly held view that the ice cap is shrinking as the planet heats up. They claim that the ice cap is actually getting thicker. As the sea warms up, the usually very dry air becomes moist. The water vapour in the air turns to snow and snow layers add to the layers of ice inland. So although the ice sheets of Antarctica are receding towards the South Pole, they are also growing higher, and this might actually offset the threat of rising sea levels. In support of this more optimistic view, some studies suggest that numbers of fur seals and emperor penguins have actually increased.

Humans in Antarctica

So far, human contact with the Antarctic has not posed a threat to the wildlife there. Humans have never established settlements in Antarctica. Researchers are allowed to spend time on the continent but there are rarely more than about 400 people living there at any one time. In 2007, about 37,000 tourists went to Antarctica for very brief visits, never staying overnight. Antarctica remains the last true wilderness on earth.

However, in 2008 an aircraft runway opened. Although it is intended for transporting research parties and their equipment, it may only be a matter of time before tourist trips are arranged. In 2007 Japanese whaling ships entered the area with the intention of hunting whales, claiming it was for scientific purposes. Like other

wildernesses, Antarctica may have reserves of oil or valuable minerals. Mining and oil companies may be tempted to exploit these in the decades to come. Commerce and tourism are likely to bring humans into increasing contact with the Antarctic in the future, to the probable cost of its flora and fauna.

An Airbus A319 jet sits on the ice runway waiting to collect scientists from the Australian Research Centre in Antarctica. The scientists have been studying the effects of climate change on the continent.

DEBATE

You are in charge

Your school is arranging a trip to the Antarctic. Before you decide to join them, you should consider the following:

- This isn't like a trip to an African wildlife reserve, for example, where local people and wildlife benefit from well-managed ecotourism. Antarctica has no locals to benefit.

- Every footstep on the Antarctic surface can cause damage, every dumped piece of waste from passing ships will pollute the sea.

- We don't know how long Antarctica will remain as undamaged as it is now. This may be your only opportunity to visit.

Should you go? Research some ways in which your visit to Antarctica could do as little damage as possible.

Glossary

acidification The process of becoming acid.

algae Very simple plants that have no stems or leaves but which photosynthesize (use sunlight as a source of energy).

amphibians Animals that can live both in water and on land.

aquatic Water based.

bottom trawling A fishing method that involves towing trawl nets along the sea floor.

carrion The rotting flesh of a dead animal.

cash crops Crops that farmers grow to sell rather than for their own consumption.

critically endangered Describing a species whose numbers have fallen so low that there is a strong chance that it will become extinct.

cull Reduce the numbers of a species by killing some.

ecological zone An area where a particular kind of ecology exists, such as savannah or coral reef.

ecologists Scientists who study ecosystems.

ecosystems All the plants and animals in an area that depend upon one another and their environment for food and shelter.

ecotourism A form of tourism that aims to minimize ecological damage to the natural environment.

endangered At risk of being wiped out.

exploit Use or develop something in order to gain a benefit.

extinct Describing a species of plant or animal that once existed but that has died out.

fauna All the animal life of a region.

flora All the plant life of a region.

fodder Plants that are grown for animal food.

food chain A hierarchy of living things, each of which feeds on the one below.

Greenpeace An international organization that takes non-violent direct action to protect the environment.

habitat The natural conditions and environment of an animal or plant.

humidity The amount of moisture in the air.

Ice Age One of several periods in earth's history when temperatures fell worldwide and large areas of the earth's surface were covered with ice sheets.

inbreeding The mating of closely related individuals of a species.

indigenous Plants or animals that are native to a place.

invasive species Non-native species of plants or animals that out-compete native species in a specific habitat.

krill A tiny marine creature similar to a shrimp.

logging Cutting down trees to sell the wood.

long-line fishing A commercial fishing technique that uses hundreds or even thousands of baited hooks hanging from a single long line.

marine Of the sea.

open-cast mining Extracting metals or minerals from the ground by removing surface layers rather than by making tunnels underground.

pollutants Any substances that when introduced to an environment damage the health of the organisms that live there.

predators Animals that eat other animals.

quota Limitations that have been imposed on the quantity of something.

savannah A grassy plain with few trees, in tropical and subtropical regions.

scavenger An animal that eats the dead remains and wastes of other animals and plants.

species A class of organism containing individuals that resemble one another and may interbreed.

sustainable A way of life that exploits natural resources without destroying the ecological balance of a particular area.

viruses Micro-organisms that can infect a plant or animal and cause disease.

Further Information

Books

Encyclopedia of Endangered Animals by Amy-Jane Beer, Pat Morris and others (Grange Books, 2005)

Endangered Species: Our Impact on the Planet by Malcolm Penny (Wayland, 2001)

Endangered Wildlife on the Brink of Extinction by George C McGavin (Cassell, 2006)

Green Alert! Threatened Habitats by Uma Sachidhanandam (Raintree, 2004)

100 Animals to See Before they Die by Nick Garbutt (Bradt, 2007)

Precious Earth: Wildlife in Danger by Jen Green (Chrysalis Children's Books, 2003)

Rainforests in Danger by Moira Butterfield (Franklin Watts, 2004)

Websites

www.endangeredspecie.com
An extensive site with information about individual endangered plants and animals. It includes a children's section and lots of links to other organizations.

www.kidsplanet.org
This website contains a long list of endangered animals with lots of information about each one, suggestions for getting involved, the issue of animal adoption, and quizzes.

www.nwf.org
A website with information on conservation of American endangered species.

www.wcs.org/international/Asia
A website with a map of the Asian region and pages for each of the countries, showing wildlife conservation work.

www.savetherainforest.org
An informative website with information about the rainforest and the consequences of its loss.

www.greenpeace.org/international/ campaigns/oceans
A section of the Greenpeace website which explains the consequences of the damage being done to the world's oceans.

www.coolantarctica.com
A website dedicated to Antarctica, with photographs, news and facts.

Debate Panel answers

Page 11:
You could look into other ways of making money from the forest. Ecotourism is a possibility. Other options include finding buyers for rainforest products such as medicines or brazil nuts. Growing crops in the shade of the outer forest is another way of making some cash for the community. Fair Trade organizations also sell textiles or other handicrafts for local communities, investing as much as possible of the profit back into the village.

Page 17:
Many big engineering projects have been prevented when sufficient numbers of people oppose them. If it can be shown that a species of plant or animal will be critically endangered by engineering work, then the work may be halted to allow a study to be carried out. An Internet or national press campaign can be very effective. Organizations such as the World Wildlife Fund can put pressure on countries whose funds are assisting the development. A famous movie star or some other international personality could also draw attention to your cause.

Page 23:
Environmental groups might support the request from Inuit groups to allow them to increase their catch. The Inuit hunt in small boats and catch only as much as they need or as their countries' quotas allow. Environmental groups would oppose plans by other whale-hunting countries. Other countries have alternative food sources and, while whale numbers may be increasing, we have no way of knowing how sustainable modern methods of whaling are. Whales are slow to reach adulthood and begin breeding. Whale-watching businesses would point out the economic value of high whale populations. They could suggest that Japan or Norway might make more money out of the 90 or so years of an individual whale's life than from killing and eating it.

Page 33:
It would certainly help to ban people from certain corridors of forest regularly used by migrating elephants. This would greatly reduce the risk to elephants and humans. So that elephants and humans don't need to compete for water supplies, deep wells could be built in villages close to elephant routes. Occasionally rogue elephants attack humans for no reason. Local authorities should deal with such situations as a matter of urgency to prevent villagers taking matters into their own hands.

Page 39:
This is a difficult issue. Many would argue that people should be able to use the country's wildlife areas. Raising the entrance fees might mean that only the rich could afford to use the parks. Closing the parks altogether might turn many people against the idea of wildlife reserves. Some compromises might be:

- Build stable, fenced walking routes.
- Recruit more park rangers and impose bigger fines for littering.
- Ban pets from the park.
- Limit access to highly popular areas such as rivers.
- Strictly control fishing to preserve fish stocks and river banks.

Page 45:
There are several arguments in favour of going. The more people that see the stunning landscapes of the Antarctic, the more chance there is of people understanding the importance of protecting it against the bigger threats of oil and mineral exploitation and permanent settlements. Tourism brings in useful income to countries in the South Atlantic, giving those countries nearest to Antarctica an incentive to protect it. You could check which company is organizing your trip and make sure that they have a good reputation. You might organize your fellow travellers and inform them about how to do the least damage while they are there: take nothing that you don't intend to bring back; don't touch animals or plants or remove anything.

Index

Page numbers in **bold** refer to illustrations.